FINDING AUSTIN'S GRANDFATHER

FINDING MY AUSTRALIAN GRANDFATHER

Douglas Johnstone

Copyright © 2017 Douglas Johnstone

The moral right of the author has been asserted.

Apart from any fair dealing for the purposes of research or private study, or criticism or review, as permitted under the Copyright, Designs and Patents Act 1988, this publication may only be reproduced, stored or transmitted, in any form or by any means, with the prior permission in writing of the publishers, or in the case of reprographic reproduction in accordance with the terms of licences issued by the Copyright Licensing Agency. Enquiries concerning reproduction outside those terms should be sent to the publishers.

Matador
9 Priory Business Park,
Wistow Road,
Kibworth Beauchamp,
Leicestershire. LE8 0RX
Tel: (+44) 116 279 2299
Email: books@troubador.co.uk
Web: www.troubador.co.uk/matador

ISBN 978 1785899 454

British Library Cataloguing in Publication Data.
A catalogue record for this book is available from the British Library.

Printed and bound by CPI Group (UK) Ltd, Croydon, CR0 4YY
Typeset in 11pt Adobe Garamond Pro by Troubador Publishing Ltd, Leicester,

Matador is an imprint of Troubador Publishing Ltd

"DEDICATED TO THE MOTHERS, WIVES, SWEETHEARTS, SISTERS AND CHILDREN OF THE MEN OF THE ANZAC FORCES 1914-1918".

CONTENTS

Acknowledgements	ix
Tentative Enquiries	1
Making the Connection	6
Three Brothers go to War	9
Marriage and Life in England	24
Returning Home	27
A Wonderful Email	33
Going to Australia	38
Anzac Day 2015	44
Grandfather's Latter Years	52
The Trail Leads to Scotland	57

ACKNOWLEDGEMENTS

This story would never have been told without the support of my family. My wonderful wife, Lorraine, encouraged me when I doubted myself. My cousin, Anne, whose tireless work, filled in the gaps and traced my uncle Archie and my grandfather. My brother-in-law, Jim, who had a 'mad' punt on Leicester City winning the Premiership in 2016 and winning at odds of 5000-1, which helped to finance the publication of this book. My mum, of course, for her unconditional love.

I am especially grateful to two special families in Australia. Nick and Ann Lincoln, who preserved my grandfather's documents when there was no one to claim them. And, Brian and Judy Dunn, for safeguarding my grandfather's military possessions.

I would like to thank the Australian Government for making available the *National Archives of Australia* and *Australian War Memorial* websites, which are free and accessible to everyone. They provide so much fascinating and vital information on the Australians who have helped shape their country and I definitely recommend anyone to take a look at them.

I would also like to thank the staff at my publishers, Matador, whose expertise and advice was invaluable in this book being produced.

Finally, I would like to thank my niece Clare, who has brought into this world my grandfather's first great great grandchild, Rainbow, on the 8th August 2016.

Douglas Johnstone

TENTATIVE ENQUIRIES

We never knew our paternal grandfather, Thomas Johnstone, and our father would never discuss him, even when pressed. The little information we learned of him was that he was an Australian who had met our grandmother, May Wood, at a military hospital in Leicester, England, while recovering from injuries sustained during the First World War. They fell in love, married and had their first child, Archie, in 1926. But, Thomas returned to Australia in 1929, taking Archie with him, leaving my grandmother pregnant with my father, Roy, in Leicester.

Our father, probably feeling deserted by his father, did not show any desire to want to find out about him. But, my sister, brother and I had always wondered about him. What kind of person was he? What did he look like? Which part of Australia was he from? Who were his family? What had happened to him and Archie? Were they still alive?

My sister, Yvonne, had tried to bring up the subject with our father several times but he always refused to discuss the matter. Our grandmother was a kindly, softly spoken Edwardian lady born in 1892 to a hosiery/hat shopkeeper.

I do not think she knew what to make of her boisterous, unruly grandchildren, and my memories of her are vague. I cannot remember her being overtly affectionate towards us and for birthdays and each Christmas we always received Premium Bonds. I do not even remember having an actual conversation with her or sharing a joke. May Johnstone died in 1975 and my mother recalls my father getting rid of most of her personal belongings and papers. When my father died in 1991 there were few personal mementoes of hers, except for a small wooden box of black and white photographs.

Although I had often wondered who my grandfather was I had no idea of where to start. I had never asked my grandmother or father about themselves or their past and now it was too late. Making tentative enquiries with my mum I found from my dad's birth certificate that his father was Thomas Wallace Johnstone, a Hosiery Salesman of 446 Hinckley Road, Leicester. My parent's marriage certificate records him as Wallace Johnstone, a Salesman. It did not seem a lot to go on.

Fortunately, in the box of photographs there was a Holy Communion book of my grandmother's, which was given to her on her confirmation on March 26th 1909 at St Nicholas Church, Leicester. It seemed to me to be a nice possession but insignificant. I told Lorraine, my wife, about my desire to discover my grandfather and she said that it was great idea. I explained that I did not know where to start and she said, "You need to go to the records office."

On the 25th March 2014 we both went to the Leicester Records Office. It is situated in an old school building, built

*My father, in his National Service Uniform,
with my grandmother.*

over a hundred years ago, and feels a bit stuffy and intimidating when you enter. With Lorraine's encouragement I found the church records for St Nicholas Church. The original documents, regardless of quality, have been preserved on microfiche, and were very accessible to look at on VDU screens. I started at the marriage records for 1914 and I immediately felt a burst of joy as I recognised the name of my great uncle, Arthur Jackson Wood. He was my grandmother's elder brother, though I had never met him as my mother and father had lost touch with him. The marriage certificate recorded:

> *Arthur Jackson Wood; bachelor age 24; occupation Architect; residence 54 St Nicholas Street; father John Wood, Hatter and Hosier, married Evelyn Ada Barnett, spinster age 27; residence 49 Guthlaxton Street; father Charles Barnett, Gardener on 15th October 1914.*

Tingling with excitement, I realised I was discovering an actual event from history which directly related to me. It appears to be such a minor thing but I felt like a big game hunter who had just 'bagged' an elephant or tiger. Could I dare think that I may find my grandparent's marriage certificate and discover who they were? I patiently looked through the subsequent documents with growing anticipation and then came up with the marriage certificate of my grandparents. It records:

> *Thomas Wallace Johnstone; bachelor age 29; occupation Professional Soldier on Active Service; residence 262 Hinckley Road; father Thomas Watt Johnstone (deceased); Commercial Traveller, married May Wood; spinster age 27; occupation not recorded; residence 54 St Nicholas Street; father John Wood, Hatter on 17th June 1919.*

It was with relief to confirm my grandfather was a soldier and so the rest of the family story may be true, though there was no indication of his nationality. I could not go any further with the records office, I needed to go onto the internet.

Thomas and May's marriage certificate.

MAKING THE CONNECTION

It was the 100th anniversary of the beginning of the First World War and the ancestry websites were abundant with advertising to help with researching one's ancestry. I logged onto a particular site, and signed up for a 7 day trial. Unfortunately, I drew a blank with "Thomas Wallace Johnstone", but I did find information on a "Thomas Watt Johnstone". He was born in Glasgow, Scotland, in 1850 and died in Werribee, Victoria, Australia in 1918. He married Blanche Wallace in 1886 and they had four children, Thomas Watt Johnstone (born South Yarra, Victoria in 1889); Alice Blanche Johnstone (born 1891); Donald Wallace Johnstone (born 1893); and Archibald Alan Johnstone (born 1895). The birth year of the eldest son would correspond with that of my grandfather's and he may have adopted his mother's maiden name when he married my grandmother.

But this was still all speculation, so I turned to the wonderful *Australian War Memorial* website to see if Thomas had actually fought in the First World War.

Typing in the name "Thomas Watt Johnstone" through the *Search for a person* search engine on the website I came upon the Embarkation Rolls record for Thomas. These were the ship's passenger manifests of every soldier who left Australia to fight in the First World War. It showed that he had indeed joined the Australian Imperial Force as a private and had left Melbourne on 19th October, 1914. It gave his next of kin as his mother Mrs B. Johnstone of 32 Council Street, Clifton Hill, Victoria, and recorded his occupation as a clerk and woodworker. Though his father was still alive when Thomas enlisted, he had put his mother down as his next of kin, suggesting conflict between him and his father. This would explain why he had adopted his mother's maiden name, when in England.

I then went on the *National Archives of Australia* website to see if I could find Thomas' war records. I must add that both these Australian websites are free and the amount of information they have available is astonishing. The website gave me access to Thomas' war service record and I discovered that Thomas had fought in Gallipoli, then in France from 1916 until the end of the war, and had actually won the Military Cross, a decoration only awarded to officers. I also discovered that Thomas' two brothers, Archibald and Donald, had also enlisted in the AIF but had been killed in action in France.

My maternal grandfather, William Allcroft, had also fought in the First World War with the Lancashire Fusiliers and though was taken as a prisoner-of-war in March 1918, he had survived the conflict. I was fortunate in that I did not know of any relatives who had been killed in either of the world wars. If Thomas was my grandfather, then it meant that two of my great-uncles had been killed in the war. This hit home to me that two of my relatives may have paid the ultimate sacrifice on active service, an emotion I had never had to experience before. I half wanted to discover that

Thomas was not my grandfather. Obviously, I still did not have concrete evidence that he was. I still needed to connect Thomas with my grandmother.

Then late in the evening of 4th April, 2014, while browsing through Thomas' war records on the NAA website I noticed an entry for 6/7/16. It read, *"5 North Genl. Hosp. Leicester – Wds severe G.S.W. R. Thigh – England."* Wow! This was it! He really had been wounded and sent to Leicester to recover. I had found my grandfather.

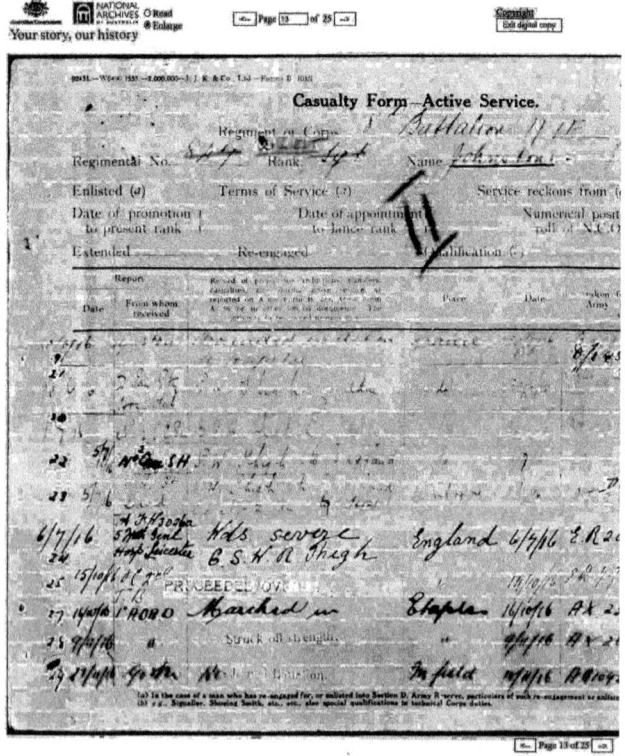

Thomas' war service record showing that he was sent to Leicester Military Hospital.

THREE BROTHERS GO TO WAR

Looking further in the National Archives of Australia records I found that my grandfather, Thomas, had joined up to fight on 7th September 1914, after his younger brother, Donald, had signed up on 22nd August. Their youngest brother, Archibald, joined up on the 7th May, 1915. It is difficult to imagine the desire to fight in a war half way around the world, but even though they had been born in Australia, each brother had put down their nationality as British when they signed up. Their father had been born in Glasgow, Scotland, but had emigrated when aged three, and their mother had been born in Australia. Thomas was a clerk, Donald a Grocer, and Archibald was also a clerk.

I also found on the website a very poignant photograph of an Australian soldier. It was a portrait photograph of Archibald Allan Johnstone.

The writing at the bottom right side of the photograph reads, "Yours sincerely Archi A Johnstone 25/3/17."

Beneath the photograph it read:

"PHOTOGRAPHER *Ramsden*
PLACE MADE *United Kingdom: England, Leicestershire*

Finding my Australian Grandfather

Archibald Johnstone, photograph taken on leave in Leicester.

Date made *c 1917*

Description *Studio portrait of 2402 Private (Pte) Archibald Alan Johnstone, 14th Battalion. A clerk from Clifton Hill, Vic prior to enlistment, Pte Johnstone embarked with the 7th Reinforcements from Melbourne on RMS Persia on 10 August 1915. Later promoted to Sergeant, he died on 20 September 1918, aged 23, of wounds received in action, and was buried in the Hancourt British cemetery, France. Two brothers also served in the AIF. 738 Corporal Donald*

Wallace Johnstone, 5th Battalion, was killed in action on 11 December 1916 and 847 Lieutenant Thomas Watt Johnstone MC, 8th Battalion, returned to Australia on 22 August 1919."

I recognised the name of the photographer, it was taken by Ramsden of 63 Granby Street, Leicester, which was the name on many of the photos of my grandmother's family. This was my great uncle Archibald Johnstone, he must have visited my grandmother while on leave in England. My mum was an only child and my dad, for all intents and purposes, was an only child too. So, to see a photograph of my great uncle was emotional to say the least.

Through the AWM website, I found that Donald served with the 5th Battalion Australian Imperial Force (AIF), his service number of 738 showing that he was one of the first Australians to enlist. His battalion left Melbourne on the 21st October 1914 aboard the troop transport ship HMAT *Orvieto*. Thomas enlisted in the 8th Battalion AIF with the service number of 847, embarking from Melbourne on the 19th October 1914 aboard the HMAT Benalle. The AIF was shipped to Egypt for army training, learning how to become soldiers. Thomas and Donald took part in the landings in Gallipoli on 25th April 1915 and fought throughout the Gallipoli campaign. The campaign was the brainchild of Winston Churchill to break the stalemate of the trench warfare in Europe and to aid Russia against the Turks. On paper the plan was simple, to capture Constantinople and take Turkey out of the war.

Though the Allies had managed to establish a foothold on

Finding my Australian Grandfather

Thomas, standing right, in Egypt.

the Gallipoli peninsula, they had to dig in unable to advance further. The Allied commanders had badly planned the operation and with dogged stubbornness the two opposing armies fought a grinding campaign with the Turkish army refusing to yield any more ground.

According to his war records, Donald was wounded at Gallipoli and sent back to Egypt on 11th August 1915, then rejoined his platoon on the 18th September. Archibald had left Melbourne on 10th August aboard the *RMS* Persia as part of the 7th Reinforcements for the 14th Battalion AIF. I would later be given a flyer, produced aboard ship, promoting the final of a boxing tournament for the weights 9st. 6lb. between RONALD v. JOHNSTONE on the boat deck on the evening of 3rd September 1915. Unfortunately, I do not know the result of the fight.

The 7th Reinforcements arrived in Gallipoli on the 1st November when the 14th Battalion took over the stretch of trench named *Durrant's Post* from the 28th Battalion, north of Anzac's Cove. So from November all three brothers were fighting on the Gallipoli peninsular. Whether they were able to meet up and swap news I do not know.

The Allies had to finally admit that they could not win the campaign and evacuated the troops in December 1915. The Australians had proven their fighting ability to the British hierarchy, though they had not won the campaign, they had not been defeated either. The Australians were sent to Europe to join the Allies fighting on the Western Front in March 1916, Thomas, Donald and Archibald were amongst them.

Thomas was badly wounded on the eve of the Somme offensive. The war diary for the AIF 8th Battalion records, "29/6/16 Messines Sector. Arrangements for gas ready but wind unfavourable. Our trenches heavily shelled by 5.9 and minnewifers, particularly sector 135. Casualties 5 killed, 24 wounded." No casualties were recorded for the 30th June, so I assume Thomas was one of the 24 recorded as being wounded on the 29th June. He was evacuated and found himself in the 5th Northern military hospital in Leicester, England, where he met my grandmother.

Unfortunately, how they met and how their romance flourished is not known. There is no correspondence of theirs and my grandmother never spoke of her courtship with Thomas. But love blossomed before Thomas had to return to the front in France in October 1916, rejoining his battalion who were still engaged in the Battle of the Somme. By this time, May's brother Arthur Wood had been conscripted into the Royal Engineers and one of her cousins, William Wood Gibbins, a Sergeant in the Royal Munster Fusiliers, had been killed (September 3rd 1916) on the Somme.

The Battle of the Somme had commenced on the 1st July 1916, and the Allies suffered the worst casualty rate ever experienced on a single day in battle by a British army. The battle was finally called off in November with 623,900

Young Thomas shortly after enlisting.

Three Brothers go to War

Allied casualties. Donald Johnstone was one those casualties, with a gunshot wound to the neck on the 25th July 1916 and needed to be transferred to Rouen for treatment. He rejoined his unit on 3rd August and was promoted to corporal on the 6th August. On the 17th August he was wounded again from a shell blast. Suffering from shell concussion and abrasions to his back he had to be sent to England to recover. He was treated at the military hospital at Becketts Park in Leeds and convalesced at Parham Downs. But, by November he was deemed able to return to his unit in France. He was killed in action near Flers on 11th December 1916. He was buried with due respect by the army and later reinterned, after the war, in the Beaulencourt British cemetery at Ligny-Thilloy in France.

In August 1916 Archibald was recommended for the Military Medal along with Privates Charles Cox, James Cumisky and H.A. Dobie by Lt. Col. Dare for their actions

Archibald mentioned in despatches.

at Pozieres. "These men continuously carried messages to and from firing line under heavy Artillery fire on nights 8/9th and 12/13th August. They, also, gave valuable assistance as guides to Artillery and other Officers who required them."

Archibald was, probably, allowed furlough in England which is when he visited Leicester and had his photograph taken, he signed it on 25th March 1917. On the 20th April 1917 Archibald was promoted to the rank of Sergeant.

In May 1917 Thomas was ordered to attend Officer Cadet Training in Oxford, England. This rise through the ranks was an indication of the lack of a class-culture in the Commonwealth armies and recognition for his devotion to duty. He was appointed 2nd Lieutenant in September, exactly three years since enlisting as a private in the AIF, and returned to France in October 1917.

During January 1918, Archibald's battalion was bombarded by Mustard Gas shells for fourteen consecutive days. Newton Wanliss, in his book *The History Of The Fourteenth Battalion, AIF* (1929), described what it was like in the trenches at this time, "The weather was cold and frosty, and there was not sufficient sunshine to enable the gas to get away. The result was that dugouts, support and communication trenches were reeking with it… As a result of the gas bombardments 17 officers and upwards of 250 men were evacuated, in addition to a large number evacuated sick from climatic and others reasons. The gas was of the ordinary mustard variety, and caused some of the evacuated to be returned to Australia. The great majority, however, returned after a comparatively brief absence to the unit… A battalion officer found several men at daybreak one morning coughing and evidently badly gassed. 'Why don't you report to the R.M.O.,' he queried; 'it means a Blighty for you.' 'Well,' retorted a gassed sergeant, 'so many have gone that if we report there will not be enough men left to do the fatigue work – the outposts will starve, and that means that the Battalion for the first time will not be able to do its proper time in the line. It will be recalled.'… This incident is a striking tribute to that intense unit pride and feeling of comradeship which were such outstanding features in the A.I.F." (pp. 260-261).

Archibald was one of the casualties. He was sent to The Princess Christian Military Hospital at Englefield Green, Surrey to be treated for Mustard Gas poisoning. His symptoms were recorded by the doctor at The Princess Christian Military Hospital, *"Mustard Shell Gas, Gassed in France 30/1/18. Symptoms. conjunctivitis right eye, lung inflamed, sore throat, cough, no vomiting, no burns, voice improving."* He was admitted into The Princess Christian Hospital on the 8th February and then transferred to Harefield Park, Middlesex on the 13th February, then discharged on the 20th February. Archibald was allowed leave to recuperate in England before being sent back to his unit in France in April 1918. Just like Donald, he was determined to return to his unit and his comrades despite his fear that his luck was running out.

Thomas was appointed Battalion Intelligence Officer on the 1st May, 1918, and in August took part in the action for which he was awarded the Military Cross. His commanding officer records: *"For conspicuous gallantry and devotion to duty during the attack North of ROSIERES on the 9/8/18. Lieut. Johnstone as Battalion Intelligence Officer did invaluable work throughout the operation, reconnoitring forward under heavy machine fire, maintaining direction and establishing liaison with flanking units. When this line was held up by fierce direct machine gun fire, this officer moved across the whole front assisting to link companies up. He then went forward at great personal risk and located the position of the German machine*

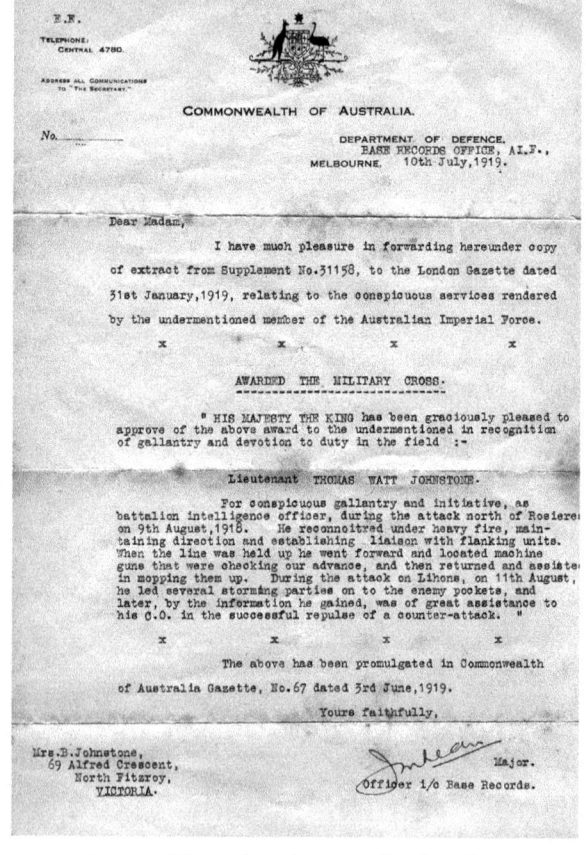

Letter to Thomas' mother regarding him being awarded the Military Cross

guns that were firing on our advance and checking it. Returning to our lines, he assisted to organise parties to mop same up, going with the parties himself and directing them as to the best means of approach and attack. During the attack on LIHONS on the 11/8/18 Lieut. Johnstone again distinguished himself by gallantry and devotion to duty. He did splendid work helping to get the battalion on the 'hopping off' line successfully. He maintained direction throughout the advance as well as leading several storming parties on to pockets of the enemy. When the enemy counter-attack developed and the situation in portion of the line became obscure, Lieut. Johnstone proceeded to the spot although the enemy has entered the line, gained a complete grip of the situation and was able to advise his C.O. and the company commanders the location and strength of the enemy, enabling the company commanders to organise his counter-attacking party and restore the situation."

The Allies had been on the offensive since late July driving the German army back all the time, with the Australian forces leading the way. The exhausted 8th Battalion was relieved on the 27th August and Thomas was allowed leave on the 31st August. He returned to the UK and most probably Leicester. It may have been on this leave that he proposed to my grandmother. But, with the end of the war a mere two months away, tragic news would await Thomas when he returned to his unit in France from furlough.

On the 20th September 1918 Archibald was hit by shrapnel to his arms, legs and back as a shell exploded close to his position. He was aged 23 years and 9 months, the same age as his brother, Donald, when he was killed. E.J. Rule, who served with Archibald in the 14th Battalion, described

Thomas, when he became an officer.

his death in his book *Jacko's Mob (1999)*, "…the Hun also got Sergeant-Major Johnstone, one of the finest lads I knew. He was torn about awfully, but he smiled through it all, and when not able to talk he would wink at us. He died back in the dressing-station after lingering a couple of hours." Archibald is buried at Hancourt British Cemetery in France.

With the war nearing its end, a lot of Thomas' comrades

who left Australia with him, at the start of the war, were now being allowed to return home and to their families for the first time in four years. The battalion's war diary for October 3rd, 1918 recorded, *"Lieut. L.C. McGINN and 40 O.R. (1914 men) marched out to FLIXECOURT to embus for BRAY en route to AUSTRALIA."* The 8th Battalion were relieved by the 118th American Regiment on the 23rd September and Thomas, as Intelligence Officer, remained behind to advise the Americans. Thomas, also, had paperwork to catch up on. The nature of the war had resulted in an unprecedented number of soldiers being recorded as 'Missing in Action' and families were desperate to discover the fates of their loved ones, their bodies were never found. One such request which Thomas had to respond to regarded Lance Corporal Chitty.

Thomas replied:

"France 5-10-'18. Ref. yours of 22-5-18. Regret very much that I have not replied to your request over this. Came across your letter when going through my papers this morning. Please accept my apologies.

"Re 2341 Pte. Chitty S.B. This man was in my Company while at Ypres. On the night 25/26/27th October 1917, he was killed by a shell on the field, while coming out after being relieved. I fancy it was on night of 25th about 11pm. Am not really certain but it was one of these three. I saw the man killed. He was only about 10 feet in front of me. I could not stay to look for his body, had some 40 to 50 men with me, I was the only officer there. We were under a heavy barrage at the time. Hope you understand the situation in which I was placed.

Finding my Australian Grandfather

Donald Johnstone's grave on the battlefield.

I knew Chitty from the time he joined the 8th Battalion. Was of a cheerful, happy nature, reliable and a clean living man. Now I remember, he was a Lance Corporal not a private. Regret that I could not see the man buried, but I honestly think the poor lad was blown to pieces. He simply disappeared into thin air. Don't inform his people of this last paragraph, please. If I can help to clear up any more missing etc, will be pleased to do so for you. Chitty was a man of about 5ft 7 or 8 in height, slightly round shoulders, not much. Dark complexion, dark eyes, dark hair. Perhaps I am slightly wrong, don't think so. Am certain this is the man though of whom you are seeking information.

Yours sincerely, Wallace Johnstone Lieut. 8th Battalion, AIF."

The war finally ended on 11th November 1918, leaving Thomas the only surviving brother. With no correspondence of Thomas' we can never know what his thoughts and mental state were in the aftermath of the war. As a Lieutenant, Thomas would have had to stay on in Europe in the army to finish off all the paperwork which required completing. Anyway, he had other business back in England to address.

MARRIAGE AND LIFE IN ENGLAND

On June 10th 1919, King George V came to Leicester to thank its town folk for their sacrifice during the war. In a major ceremony, along with others, Thomas was presented with the Military Cross from the king. The local newspaper, *The Leicester Daily Mercury*, in its report on the occasion reported, "Lieutenant Johnstone was given a special word by the King, who asked him if he were soon going back to Australia." Seven days later, Thomas married my grandmother. No one in my family had any idea that Grandma May had married a war hero. The local newspaper also published a photograph of them outside St Nicholas church, with the headline: "Australian Officer's Wedding in Leicester." May's parents, John and Sarah Wood are on Thomas' left, while May's brother Arthur and his wife Ada, are on her right.

Underneath the photograph it read: "At St. Nicholas's Church on Tuesday, Miss May Wood, daughter of Mr. and Mrs. John Wood… 282, Hinckley-road, was married to Lieut. T.W. Johnstone, M.C. (AIF). Lieut. Johnstone received the M.C. from the King at the Investiture at De Montfort Hall. Our photograph shows the bridal party after the ceremony."

Marriage and Life in England

*My grandparents on their wedding day,
outside St. Nicholas Church, Leicester.*

His army records show that on the 22nd August 1919 he left the Army and returned to Australia, the first time he had visited his home since the outbreak of the war. During which time, he had lost his two brothers and his father had also passed away in 1918. I do not know whether he took my grandmother with him. Obviously, he returned to England to settle into married life.

Thomas worked for his father-in-law in his hatters/hosiery shop and the newly married couple lived in the flat above the shop in 54 St Nicholas Street, Leicester. Archie was born on 24th November 1925, whom I presume Thomas named after his youngest brother. There are a few photographs of Thomas and May on family holidays, with John and Sarah Kate Wood.

Finding my Australian Grandfather

My Uncle Archie, before being taken to Australia.

It is obvious, from the photographs that everyone doted on Archie. But, for whatever reason, the marriage failed and Thomas felt the need to return to Australia.

RETURNING HOME

I had been told that Thomas returned to Australia in 1929 and looking on another Australian website found the passenger list for the Aberdeen & Commonwealth liner SS Jervis Bay, which left Southampton on 1st May 1929 bound for Sydney. Amongst the passengers were Thomas and Archie. It also had their address for the redirection of correspondence as: "c/o Commonwealth Bank, Melbourne." Thomas had booked himself and Archie on an Australian bound ship for the month before but had cancelled the passage to go on the next ship. By this time, Thomas and May had separated and my mother informed me that May had told her that Thomas had taken Archie out one day and did not return. I searched the local newspapers for that period, thinking there would be a report on Thomas's absconding with Archie, but there are no reports at all. My father, Roy, was born on the 9th August 1929.

I had also found that Thomas' mother Blanche Johnstone had arrived in England in 1925, when May was expecting Archie. Blanche had put down my grandparent's address, 54 St Nicholas Street, Leicester, as her forwarding address. She remained in England until after my father was born. This asks more questions regarding her arrival and what her daughter-in-law felt about having her with them. Blanche Johnstone

Finding my Australian Grandfather

```
            ABERDEEN & COMMONWEALTH LINE.
LIST OF PASSENGERS' ADDRESSES.   S.S.   JERVIS BAY          Voyage 3
 Left SOUTHAMPTON    Date 1st MAY '29  Arrived SYDNEY    Date
 Commander A.V.RICHARDSON  Surgeon W.H.FRAYNE    Purser G.D.DENHOLM

Ticket                                                Address for
 No.         Name           From    To           Redirection of Correspondence

   Adams        Miss K.V.M.   Soton Sydney  C/o Bush Nursing Assccn:Sydney.
 R—Archibald   Mr.D.                        C/o National Bank of Australia,
                                                                    Sydney.
   Balshaw      Mr.J.                       Takapotaki,Toa Toa,Opotiki,
                                            Bay of Plenty,New Zealand.
   Beeston      Miss E.                     C/o Bush Nursing Assccn:Sydney.
   Bickerstaff  Mr.W.                       C/o B.B.M.,Sydney.
   Bickle       Mrs.A.F.                    C/o Aberdeen & Commonwealth Line,
      "         Master Ian  (8)                                     Sydney.
      "         Master Neil (4)                       "
 R—Boddam-Whitham Mr.H.                     42 Mandulong Rd.,Moyman,N.H.W.
 R—     "         Mrs.H.                              "
   Boyne        Mr.H.C.                     132 King St.,Newtown,Sydney.
   Bradbury     Mr.A.J.                     C/o Govt:Migration Office,Sydney.
     "          Mrs.V.E.                              "
   Brues        Mr.C.N.                     C/o Mr.H.Natt,"Strathisla",
                                            Condobolin Rd.,Trundle,N.S.W.
   Butcher      Mr.G.                       C/o B.B.M.,Sydney.
   Chilton      Mr.C.                       4 Claremount St.,Royelle,Sydney.
   Coleman      Rev.T.R.                    5 Oberon Crescent,Gordon,N.S.W.
   Cook         Mrs.J.S.                    C/o Vacuum Oil Co.Pty.Ltd.
                                            Kembla Bldg.,Margaret St,Sydney.
      "         Miss M.N.    (3)                      "
   Corbett      Mr.E.                       C/o B.B.M.,Sydney.
   Cory         Mr.D.J.                                "
   Crockett     Mr.F.W.                                "
   Dougherty    Mr.R.A.R.                   C/o Mr.W.Barnhill,Namoon Farm 390
                                                          via Beeston.
   Dunnill      Mr.E.                       C/o B.B.M.,Sydney.
   Ellis        Mr.J.                       C/o Immigration Officer,Sydney.
   Evans        Mr.W.M.                     74 Rosa St.,Oatley,Sydney.
     "          Mrs.F.M.                              "
     "          Miss M.N.    (7)                      "
   Fellows      Miss I.G.                   "Ceromic",Manana Rd.,Harlwood.
   Forshaw      Mr.H.                       "Glenaeven",12 Landsdowne Road,
                                            Panesmite,N.S.W.
   Garnett      Mr.J.A.                     C/o B.B.M.,Sydney.
   Gibbs        Mr.S.                       C/o Joyce,Wetherell St,Auburn.
   Glasgow      Miss D.M.                   135 London St.,Dunedin,N.Z.
   Grant        Mr.P.D.                     C/o B.B.M.,Sydney.
   Grinsek      Miss K.                     378 Bondi Rd.,Bondi Beach,Sydney.
   Green        Mrs.A.A.                    7 Kitchener St.,Coogee.
     "          Miss D.      (2)                      "
     "          Master W.B.  (8)                      "
 R—Hall         Mr.J.                       Stewart St.,Paddington,Sydney.
 R—Hall         Mr.F.                       C/o Whare,Lanette St,Chatswood.
   Hall         Mr.R.M.                     C/o J.D.Hall,Claremount,Nimbin,
                                            Richmond River,N.S.W.
   Henderson    Mrs.H.                      79 Ryedale Rd:West Ryde,N.S.W.
   Jenks        Mr.J.W.                     Maitland Rd:Mayfield,Newcastle.
     "          Mrs.E.                                "
   Jenkin       Mr.A.C.                     C/o A.J.Jenkin,Bayswater Rd,
                                                                    Croydon.
   Johnstone    Mr.T.                       C/o Commonwealth Bank,Melbourne.
      "         Master A.    (3½)                     "
```

Passenger List for Jervis Bay.

was aboard the Largs Bay when it departed Southampton on 27th November 1929 bound for Australia, leaving my father with his mother.

My grandmother never talked about the pain of losing Archie, but I can understand her reticence in leaving her family to move halfway across the world, and it must have

28

been an agonising decision for both my grandparents. No one will ever know what heart breaking discussions went on the Johnstone household in 1929, but I now feel I know why my father felt so reluctant to discuss or want to find his father. I think that he felt deserted, left in a dreary England with his Edwardian mother, whom I remember as kindly but old fashioned. 1929 was a traumatic year for my grandmother. As well as losing her husband and son, and pregnant with my father, her father died in the September. So, my father was raised by his mother and grandmother, never having known his father or grandfathers.

I turned my research to Thomas' other sibling, his sister Alice Blanche Johnstone (born 1891; died 1960). In the box of photographs of my grandmother's there was a photograph of a beautiful lady, it was signed "Yours Lovingly Alice 1916." The name of the photographic studio stamped on the photograph was Alpha Studios, 200 Smith Street, Collingwood (Melbourne). Could this be my great aunt, sent to Thomas while he was in the trenches?

The only other information I had about her was that she married Ralph John St Paul at the Scots Church, Melbourne on 30th November 1922. I went onto the Internet and typed in "ScotsChurch" and found the church's website. I sent an email asking if they had any further information on Alice Blanche Johnstone and a few days later their archivist sent a reply. The email read,

> *"I found a baptism record for June Marie St. Paul born 6th February, 1924 and baptised by Rev Dr Alexander Marshall on 9th July, 1924. Her parents Ralph John St.*

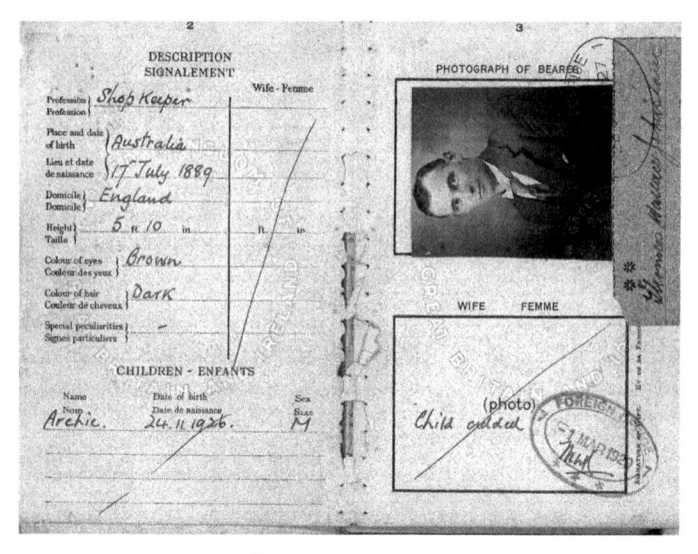

Thomas' passport, 1929.

Paul and Alice Clyde Johnstone; 97 Hodgkinson Street, Clifton Hill. I checked communicant rolls and pew rental books but could find no further records."

So, my grandfather had a niece and his sister was also as free and easy with her middle name as he was. But, try as I might I could not discover any more about June. If she had married, then I'd hoped there would be a record of her marriage at the Scots Church. If she had died a spinster then the Australian Johnstone line would die with her, and I would waste too much time and effort on a fruitless search. I reluctantly decided not to pursue this line any further. I decided that my best bet would be looking at my father's brother, Archie's line.

I managed to access Australia's Electoral Rolls (though at the time I believed it was the census records). I found that, in 1949, Archie was living with Thomas Watt Johnstone and Jean Stirling Johnstone at 11 Franklyn Street, Concord. Then in 1954, Shirley Patricia Johnstone was also living with Archie, Thomas and Jean at 11 Franklyn Street. The records only recorded the name, address and occupation of each individual. They do not record the relationship of each individual within the household, or their age, or where they were born.

So, had Thomas married Jean and was Archie married to Shirley? The British census records enable researchers to see a much clearer picture of the family members, and realised how lucky we are in this country to have these records. My mother mentioned that my grandmother had told her that she had received divorce papers, out of the blue, from Thomas' solicitors. So, it seems, my grandfather had remarried. I was pleased that he had remarried and, hopefully, was happy in his second marriage.

Thomas and Jean Johnstone then disappear from later records, I found that Archie was living at Temora Road, c/o Mrs V. Hughes. Then in 1980 he pops up as living with Isobel May Johnstone at Wombat Road in Young. So, had Archie also remarried or was this his daughter. I could only speculate. But, this was as far as I got with trying to find my grandfather and my Australian family. Thomas had probably remarried, Archie had married and had had a daughter or had just married twice. The thing I clung onto was that Isobel had the name May as her middle name. Was this because she was Archie's daughter and he had given her his mother's name?

It was so frustrating to have got this far only to find I could not go further. I now had more questions than answers, which all family researchers have told me occurs. You discover something about your ancestor only to find it brings up more unknowns. I really believed that the family line had died with Archie and his cousin June St Paul. I had gone as far as I thought I could, I sent letters to the addresses in Australia, where my ancestors had lived, explaining my story. I received no replies.

A WONDERFUL EMAIL

I had taken out another trial contract on an ancestry website, which had a lot of information on my Johnstone ancestry. I had no idea how this information had been found and my trial period was about to end, so I posted on its website my details in case the person who had also been researching the Johnstone family tree responded. It was a hurried post which I left as I was going off to London for a romantic weekend with my wife. I dared not hope for a response but had a deep down feeling that there was someone out there who was also researching the Johnstone family.

When I returned home from London, late in the evening, I went on to the message board of the website and was absolutely overwhelmed with excitement to find someone had responded. It read,

"RE: Thomas Watt Johnstone
　"Hello Douglas,
　"I have quite a bit of information on him, and I am excited to learn he had a son to carry on the Johnstone name. I know he returned from the 1st World War, his other two brothers having died in France. Both are buried in Northern France. I know he moved to NSW and married Jean Stirling Kidner, who I believe had

been married before. Thomas Watt Johnstone was my Great Uncle. I would love to know details of his death and even a photo would be appreciated. I will forward details of his birth etc. this evening. There is a lot regarding his war service on the AIF site. Kind regards, Anne."

I could hardly believe that I had discovered a close cousin. Being on opposite sides of the world corresponding with each other was difficult as I would send an email while Anne was sleeping and she would respond while I slept. The first thing I did every morning before going to work would be to look for the next email from Anne to find out what she knew about our ancestors and her responses to my many questions about herself and her family. Anne informed me that she was the granddaughter of Thomas' sister Alice, so the Australian line had not ended with June St Paul. Anne had a younger brother and sister, Michael and Kate. I, co-incidently, had one brother and one sister.

We shared what information we had on our respective grandparents and families and helped each other to fill in the gaps of our family's history. I found that Thomas' father had been born in Glasgow, Scotland, in 1850 and had come to Australia with his parents in the 1850s. Anne confirmed that he was separated from Thomas' mother Blanche Wallace Johnstone and had died in Werribee in 1918.

Anne sent me a photograph of my grandfather standing in the doorway of a hat shop. This was the shop owned by my grandmother's father, John Wood, and for whom Thomas worked after the war. It was in the flat above the shop, 54 St

Thomas outside his father-in-law's hat shop in Leicester.

Nicholas Street, Leicester, where my grandparents lived. My family believed that my great grandfather had a hat shop but had never seen a photograph of the actual shop. The building was demolished and a pretty square now occupies the space.

Anne sent me Thomas' birth certificate which she had ordered from the Australian Records Office. She had also obtained Thomas' death certificate, as well as Archie and Shirley's marriage certificate. She discovered that Archie knew he had a brother back in England but had never tried to make contact. Though Anne never knew my grandfather, she had fond memories of her grandmother Alice St. Paul (nee Johnstone), who was affectionately known as "Grandma Paulie."

I had already decided to go to Australia with the realisation that my grandfather and his brothers had fought in the First World War and was determined to be in Melbourne for the 100th Anniversary of the Anzac landings in Galipolli. I waited until Christmas Day to inform the family of my intentions, which gave me exactly four months before the Anzac Day memorial events on the 25th April 2015. My wife and mum agreed to go with me and we began to organise the trip, which a year before we had no idea we would be going on.

Anne placed a notice in the *Young Witness* newspaper for anyone who knew Archie or Isobel Johnstone. She received a reply from Nick and Anne Lincoln, who had purchased the property after Isobel had died. Archie and Isobel had run a pig farm and orchard. Archie had died before Isobel and his ashes scattered on their farm in Young. Isobel's last wish was to be buried on the farm and this is where her grave is now. They had lost touch with their families and there were no relatives to attend either of their funerals

Amazingly, the Lincolns had stored my uncle and aunt's personal effects in case any relations did turn up and sent them straightaway to Anne. One of their documents was the divorce papers of my grandparents, which Thomas had filed and sent to my grandmother. There were Thomas and his mother's passports and letters which suggested that Thomas suffered from ill-health later in life. There was also a 3rd class ship ticket for Australia arriving on 27th November 1929 for Blanche Johnstone, suggesting Thomas' mother had been in England. The Lincolns also informed Anne that there had been some World War One possessions which they had donated to a local military museum. In January Anne contacted the museum's curator who informed her that there were Thomas' dress medals and photographs in the collection and was only too happy for her to view them.

A month before we were due to go to Australia Anne emailed me to inform me that she had found out where Thomas' ashes had been scattered. Though he had died in New South Wales, someone had scattered his ashes in a garden of remembrance in Melbourne, I assume it was his son Archie.

I had found my grandfather. Though he had died many years before, I had somewhere I could pay my respects and this was going to be one of my priorities when I arrived in Australia.

Anne had done a fantastic amount of work to discover the facts about Thomas and his family in Australia. I now had a clear plan of objectives I wanted to do when in Australia. I wanted to visit the military museum in Harden, New South Wales, where Thomas' medals were being looked after. Also, the Lincoln's farm to ask them about Archie and Isobel. The Springvale Memorial Gardens where Thomas' ashes had been scattered and to be at the Anzac Day Dawn Service in Melbourne. I was now ready and couldn't wait to see what lay in store for me in the homeland of my grandfather.

GOING TO AUSTRALIA

We flew from Birmingham Airport on a warm spring evening and arrived in a cool, wet Australia a few days later. I did not feel as if I was on the other side of the world, but strangely enough, as soon as I arrived in Melbourne I felt at home, as if I had always had an affinity with it. It is a beautiful city, rich in architecture and history.

I met my cousin Anne, and her husband Barry, the very next day for lunch. I was too excited to be nervous, and though we had exchanged many, many emails over the past four months, I did wonder how we would get on. I need not have worried, as our personalities were so similar. Anne presented me with a pair of gold cufflinks which had been in the belongings of Arthur and Isobel's saved by the Lincolns and sent to Anne. They had the initials "TWJ" and had obviously been Thomas' cufflinks. Anne also gave me a photograph of Thomas in uniform, just after he had enlisted, looking young and innocent. He was twenty five when he signed up, but he looked must younger in the photograph.

The next day, Wednesday 22nd April, we went to Anne's house for her to show us the papers she had regarding the Johnstone family history, birth, marriage and death certificates which Anne had obtained during her research. She had managed to gather so much information and Anne gave me copies of everything, so that I could digest it all in my own time. It appeared that Thomas' father, who was also named Thomas Watt Johnstone, was born in Glasgow, Scotland, in 1850 and had come to Australia when his parents emigrated there soon after he was born. Their subsequent children were born in Portland Victoria, Australia. I now had solid evidence of my Scottish ancestry and I was surprised that it only went back to three generations. We left Anne late in the afternoon. I had taken up so much of Anne's time as she had so much fascinating information to show me that the time had flown by. We arranged to meet her on the Saturday for the Anzac Day Dawn Service in Melbourne.

Archie Johnstone in Australia.

Finding my Australian Grandfather

I had a lot of documents to go through, Anne had discovered the lives of our great aunts and uncles, family I had no idea I had. She also gave me everything that the Lincolns had saved of my uncle's, which included my grandfather's passport, his divorce papers, personal letters and photographs of Archie. Back in our apartment I was able to study the documents. The divorce papers, issued in the Supreme Court of Victoria on 28th February 1938, recorded Thomas Wallace Johnstone as the Petitioner and my grandmother, May Johnstone, as the Respondent. It recorded, "that the Respondent had been personally served with the Petition and Citation in this cause and that no appearance had been entered herein by or on behalf of the Respondent." Thomas was asking for the marriage to "BE DISSOLVED on the ground that the Respondent has without just cause or excuse wilfully deserted the Petitioner and without any such cause or excuse left him continuously so deserted during three years and upwards." My understanding of the argument from Thomas is that my grandmother deserted him because she refused to leave her home country and elderly parents to go with him to Australia. She was, obviously, not represented in court because she was still living in England and unable to present her case in a court the other side of the world.

Amongst the documents saved were my grandfather's marriage certificate showing he married Jean Stirling Kidner in 1938. The ties he had with England were now finally cut, he had divorced his wife in England and appeared to have given up his son in England. He had Archie and his future was in Australia. Anne was able to give me a photograph of Archie, my uncle I never had.

Thomas' plaque in Springvale's Garden Of Remembrance.

I had set aside Thursday to visit my grandfather's memorial in the Springvale Garden of Remembrance, where Anne informed me that Thomas' ashes had been scattered. The Garden of Remembrance, situated within the cemetery, remembers anyone who served in the Australian armed forces and is a beautiful and tranquil area maintained by the Office of Australian War Graves Commission. The main features are the walls on which plaques with the names of veterans are remembered, but there are also flower beds, trees and walks to enjoy. Anne had already visited the garden of remembrance and had explained exactly where to find my grandfather's plaque.

Not knowing my grandfather I cannot presume to think of how he wanted to be remembered, but someone had this plaque put up and had his ashes scattered in Springvale. This could only have been Archie and he must have done what he thought was what his father wanted. I had come all this way to find my grandfather, now I had found him and it was very emotional to be able to pay my respects to him.

Along with the information Anne was providing for me and my own research, I was beginning to piece together his life after he had left my grandmother and returned to Australia. Blanche had arrived in England on 31st August 1925 embarking from Melbourne aboard the *SS Baradine*. On the passenger list, Blanche put down 54 St Nicholas Street, Leicester as her proposed address in England. She must have been in Leicester for the birth of her first grandchild, Archie on the 24th November 1925. Though Thomas returned to Australia with Archie aboard the *Jervis Bay* in May 1929, Blanche did not leave England until 27th November 1929.

The Australian Electoral Rolls record Thomas as living with Blanche on Beach Road in Sandringham, Melbourne in 1937. Anne had informed me that Blanche had died in 1938 and then Thomas married Jean Stirling Kidner at Burwood, New South Wales on 6th September 1938. He and Jean lived in Concord, New South Wales until their deaths. Anne discovered that Jean had been born in Queensland in 1892, her parents were Alexander and Bertha McDonald. Jean had married Edward Kidner in 1910, they had four children but Edward died in 1933. How my grandfather and Jean met is unknown, but Anne informed me that Thomas and Jean both died in 1967. I was 8 years old when Thomas died and would have loved to have met him. I doubt whether he even knew he had grandchildren. It seems that Thomas and his sister, Alice, lost contact after he moved to New South Wales. Alice lived in Melbourne her whole life, and Anne still remains in the area. I, also, still live in the city where my grandmother was born.

Thomas had been a clerk when he enlisted in 1914 and after the war he went back to being a shopkeeper. He was just an ordinary man who had to do extraordinary things during the First World War and had returned to his normal life when the war finished. He had been through one of the most harrowing of wars in which millions had been killed or maimed and in which he had lost both his brothers.

But when the Second World War broke out in 1939 my grandfather again felt compelled to join up. He was fifty years old when he received his commission as a Lieutenant on 20th August 1940. He was posted to the 14th Garrison Battalion who were stationed at Hays Interment Camp, New South Wales, where Italian prisoners of war were to be confined. I think he would have preferred a more active posting but his medical examination only rated him as class II so spent the war escorting prisoners and ensuring their security. He was promoted to the rank of Captain in 1942 and returned to civilian life in 1944 due to ill-health.

ANZAC DAY 2015

It felt as if I was meant to be in Australia for the 100th anniversary of the Gallipoli Landings on the 25th April 1915 to remember all the service personnel who have sacrificed their lives for their country. It was my first real chance to represent my grandfather, Donald and Archibald, and it was important to me to have my cousin, Anne, with me.

The first remembrance services in 1916 were spontaneous ad-hoc occasions in which men, now fighting in France or continuing the fight against the Turkish army in Palastine, wanted to remember their comrades left behind on the beaches of Gallipoli. Thomas, Archibald and Donald had been sent to France, along with the majority of the Australian Imperial Force. They disembarked in Marseilles in March 1916 and then began to be integrated into the trenches of the Western Front to bolster the troops already fighting there.

It was wet and cold for Anzac Day 2015. Workers on the trams and trains come into work specially to ferry the huge number of people coming into Melbourne from the surrounding areas from early morning. People had been gathering at the Shrine of Remembrance long before the service was due to commence. Lorraine and I met Anne on

Anzac Day 2015

the steps of Flinders Street train station at 5.20am to walk the short distance for the start of the service at 6am. She had travelled by train from the suburb of Beaumaris 20 kilometres outside of Melbourne. Anne gave us both a sprig of rosemary to wear. It is traditional to wear this herb on Anzac Day because it grew wild on the peninsular of Gallipoli and is supposed to have the medicinal power to aid memory, hence for remembrance. We walked with the vast crowd of people making their way down St Kilda Road and had to stand toward the back of the crowd for the ceremony. We watched it on huge screens as people of the armed forces and relatives of those who died read excerpts from the diaries of those who landed on that fateful morning.

Anne and I after the Dawn Service at Melbourne's Shrine of Remembrance.

The Last Post was listened to in respectful silence and everyone thought of those who had landed on the beaches of Gallipoli one hundred years previously. Renditions of *Abide with Me* and *In Flanders Fields* were performed and speeches on the sacrifices made. After the ceremony the crowds dispersed for breakfast but were lining the streets of Melbourne again at 9am for the parade of servicemen and ex-servicemen, relatives, bands and vintage vehicles. 80,000 people had attended the dawn service in Melbourne and it was a privilege to have been amongst them. We went back to our apartment for breakfast with Anne and to go over more family research documents which we wanted to show each other. Later, we were able to watch live on the television the ceremonies of remembrance from Gallipoli and France because their time zones were later than that in Australia.

Anne had organised a barbeque for us to meet my Australian cousins, so the day after Anzac Day we all met up at her brother's family home. The weather had not improved, it remained wet and cold, not how I imagined an Australian barbeque would be like. It was wonderful to get to know Anne, Michael, Kate and their families, there was so much to discover and share.

The next day Lorraine and I were driving north to try to find my uncle's farm in Young, where he lived with his second wife, Isobel. On the way I wanted to visit Brian Dunn in Harden, who had set up a museum to the Australian Light Horse Brigade, and had been sent my grandfather's military possessions for the museum. It was an honour to meet Brian and his wife, and he was a most interesting chap. As well as the medals of my grandfather he had photographs and a newspaper article reporting the death of Thomas and Archibald's brother Donald. The report was from *The Herald* dated July 7, 1917. It read,

> *"FIFTH WOUND FATAL. After having been twice wounded in Gallipoli and twice in France, Corporal Donald Wallace Johnston has been killed in action. He left Australia with the first contingent. Sergeant T. W. Johnston, his brother was wounded twice in Gallipoli and once in France. Private A. W. Johnston, another brother, is also abroad. They are the sons of Mrs Johnston, Alfred Crescent, North Fitzroy."*

The article also had a photograph of Donald. Now, for the first time, I knew what Donald looked like. Donald was the first brother to be killed on 11th December 1916, but his death was not reported until July 1917. I do not know how or when his family learned of his death, I do not even know how he died. I know from his army records that he was 'killed in action' and Mr Dunn gave me the photograph of Donald's temporary headstone when he was buried 'in the field', so he may have been shot or died from shrapnel wounds.

The battalion's war diary for the 11th December reported, "1 other rank wounded. 2/Lieut. F. B. CONWAY reinforcement reported for duty." For 12th December, it reported, "1 other rank killed, 3 O. R's wounded."

Mr Dunn and his wife were so hospitable that I felt guilty that I had to rush away, but I still had to visit Ann and Nick Lincoln in Young before returning to Melbourne. Mr Dunn said that my grandfather's possessions belonged to me and

The Melbourne Herald *reporting Donald's death, July 7, 1917.*

I was so grateful to accept them. I told him that the medals belonged to the Australian people, but I would be grateful if I could take them back to Melbourne to show to Anne and then would send them back to him for the museum. He asked if I would like to see the museum and I wished I could, but it was already lunchtime and I knew we did not have enough time. We chatted about the Australian Light Horse who stayed in the Middle East after the evacuation of Gallipoli and won a major cavalry victory against the Turkish army at Beersheba which, ultimately, resulted in the defeat of Turkey. I left Brian's house jubilant with finding more about my family but sad that I could not have spent more time with him.

I now had to find my uncle's former farm. He had lived in a rural area, but this was not English rural countryside. In

England villages are perhaps a few miles apart. In Australia, homesteads are a few miles apart. We finally found Archie's old farm. Anne had informed me that he had been a telephone engineer and he had married Isobel in 1969. They then purchased the farm and Archie had become an orchardist and Isobel wanted to run a pig farm. We eventually found the farm, which isn't easy with just the address as Wombat Road. It certainly made for some colourful exchanges between the driver and his navigator.

We drove up the drive toward the Lincoln's home, which stood on the brow of a hill, and the sun shone golden above it. I felt that I was intruding and was glad that they were expecting us and came out to greet us. As usual, I felt awkward and did not know what to say. Ann and Nick then explained that Archie had already died before they had moved to Young and they had only known Isobel. They explained that Archie had asked for his ashes to be scattered on the farm when he died which Isobel did. But Isobel insisted that she wanted to be buried on her own land. Archie had had his ashes scattered on the farm, so I presume they are still together. I am sure it was Archie who took his father's ashes back to Melbourne to have them scattered at the Springvale Garden of Remembrance.

Ann and Nick gave me a photograph of Archie when he was an adult. It was the first time I had seen a photograph of Archie as an adult and his resemblance to my father is quite remarkable. They also gave me the original photograph of my great uncle Archibald in his AIF uniform. The fact that Archie had kept it meant that he felt an affinity with the uncle he was named after. I spent a few quiet moments by Isobel's graveside, even though I had never knew her she

Finding my Australian Grandfather

Isobel May Johnstone's grave.

was still my auntie. Ann explained that Isobel became too attached to her pigs refusing to have them killed and at her death was heavily in debt. I left the Lincoln's farm tinged with sadness but so grateful that they had preserved the memory and treasured mementos of my family. Archie and Isobel had died, having lost all contact with their families, so there were no family present at their funerals. Fortunately, the Lincoln's kept the possessions which they thought would be wanted by family if we ever turned up. If it had not been for them, the memories of my uncle and auntie could have been lost forever.

Unfortunately, we did not have enough time to visit all the places I wanted to visit, such as the house on Alfred Crescent in Melbourne, where the family lived during the First World War and the brother's school they attended. One of the highlights of the trip was visiting the museum within the Shrine of Remembrance. After I had returned to England I had the time to examine and collate all the information I had gathered from Australia.

GRANDFATHER'S LATTER YEARS

It was not just the photographs and medals that Ann and Nick had been able to save for us but also the old bits of correspondence of my grandfather's. When, my cousin, Anne had emailed to say that the Lincoln's had sent her letters of my grandfather's I had hoped they may have been letters sent by him to other family members expressing his thoughts and things he had done. Unfortunately, they were not as exciting or intriguing as personal letters, but they were no less important in telling the story of Thomas' latter years.

One of the photographs, which I received, was of my grandfather in a Second World War officer's uniform looking dignified and relaxed outside the Sergeant's Mess hut, most probably at the Hay Internment Camp.

He had an unremarkable Second World War having to guard prisoners of war. The only injury he received was when he fell from an observation tower. He was promoted to the rank of captain in 1942 and left the army for a second time in 1944. Again, he went back to being a salesman and worked at the store Millard's on George Street in Sydney. One of his papers saved by Ann and Nick Lincoln was his reference letter when he left the company. It read,

Grandfather's Latter Years

Thomas at Hay's Internment Camp, during WW2.

"TO WHOM IT MAY CONCERN.
This is to certify that Mr Thomas Watt Johnstone, whose signature appears below, was in our employ from November 1944 to February 26th, 1947.

POSITION HELD: Salesman in Men's Clothing Department

PERSONAL CHARACTER: Good

ATTENDANCE: Regular

> *GENERAL REPORT: Mr Johnstone has proved to be honest and trustworthy during his service with this Company. He leaves owing to a re-arrangement in our staff."*

The rest of the papers relate to his health, which was beginning to affect his ability to work. He worked at the Royal Australian Navy Armament Depot as a storeman from 1947 to 1952 but throughout this period was having to have time from work through illnesses, such as sciatica and bronchitis He received a letter from the Department of the Navy, dated 14th October 1952. It read,

> *"Dear Sir,*
> *With reference to your extended absence on sick leave I regret to inform you that as you have exceeded the maximum period of sick leave which is allowed without pay your services have been terminated as from close of business, 2nd October, 1952."*

So, after serving his country in two world wars, he was thrown on the scrapheap at the age of 62. He was, already, receiving a war pension and had been diagnosed as having osteoarthritis of the right hip and both knees. He tried to claim that his disability was due to his First World War injuries, but this was rejected by the Repatriation Commission of New South Wales. In drafts of letters Thomas wrote to the Commission to support his claim, he wrote about being injured in 1915 while fighting in Gallipoli at the trench "…Steel's Post, blown out of sap with others, by the Turks. Possibly the start of injury of right hip." He also recalled when he became a casualty in France, "I do not remember being wounded or buried in the trench at Messines in 1916. There is no doubt on my part that the injury to both the right thigh and knee joints, particularly right knee joint was caused by and at the same time as being wounded and buried by the collapsed trench. I only remember awaking at the Canadian Hospital in Boulogne, Belgium."

At the end of one of his letters, he wrote, "In conclusion, I am not in any way complaining. I think I have been helped and treated in the manner which Australia promised us, when we enlisted. I honestly believe the Osteoarthirtus, the right knee in particular was the result of war when wounded in 1916. Yours TWJ."

In 1949 he sailed to San Francisco, USA, with his wife, Jean, but I do not know for what reason. Archie married Shirley Thompson on 16th September, 1950. He put his occupation down as a Telephone Technician. The marriage certificate records his mother, May Wood, as being deceased. They were divorced in 1960.

Thomas died on the 20th June, 1967 from a stroke and pneumonia, only a few months after, his wife, Jean had died. Only one personal letter of his has survived, which expresses his emotions. It is addressed to Harold and dated 16/01/67. In it he writes,

"Just a few lines before I retire for the night! Six months alone, and my sweetheart is still in hospital. What a life to have!

I do not know what to do with my self… To begin with, Jean is coming along reasonably well. This is the main thing and really 'All' that matters, with me. Time now is 6.55. I spend all my time reading at night & feel darn miserable both day and night! Suppose, this is the 'Way' of Life!

How are you keeping? Bright and happy, I hope. Not like me, I hope."

May brought up my father in the family home on Hinckley Road in Leicester with her mother, Sarah Kate Wood. Sarah died in 1952 and my mother and father married in 1955. Free of responsibilities May moved down to the seaside town of Bournemouth. She remained faithful to Thomas and stayed a spinster for the rest of her life. She returned to Leicester in the late 1960s and died in 1975. She rests with her parents, John and Sarah Kate Wood, in Welford Road Cemetery situated opposite the military hospital where Thomas was treated in 1916. The hospital is now Leicester University, where genetic fingerprinting was pioneered by Sir Alec Jeffreys in the 1980s.

When I first walked into the Leicester Records Office in 2014 I did not know I was going to discover as much as I have about my grandfather. There are some things I would not rather have found out, but the good things far outweigh the sad ones. Finding that I had Australian cousins was the most wonderful of all.

Reflecting upon my grandfather and his actions made me realise that not only do we have to live with the consequences of our choices in life, but how others are affected by these decisions. Thomas never got to know his youngest son and his grandchildren, and we never got to know him or our uncle.

THE TRAIL LEADS TO SCOTLAND

My cousin Anne has managed to find out so much information about our Johnstone ancestors that she has been able to trace them back to where in Scotland they are from and when they left their homeland to make a new life in Australia.

Our great, great grandparents were Thomas Watt Johnstone (born 1828 in Laurieston, Stirlingshire) and Jane Logan (born 1829 in Glasgow). They married on the 15th March, 1850 at St Peter's Church in Glasgow and lived at Reform Court, 50 Commerce Street, Gorbals, Lanarkshire. Thomas and Jane had two children, Thomas Watt jnr. (born on 24th December 1850) and Elizabeth Mcdougall Johnstone (born on 1st December 1852).

I cannot imagine the reasons why they left their homeland to embark on a perilous journey to an unknown continent and future. But, on the 3rd November 1853 the young couple took their two infant children to Australia in search of a better life for themselves and their children, leaving Liverpool aboard *The Utopia*. Thomas is listed as a Blacksmith from Lanark, Scotland, aged 25 and Jane Johnstone is aged 24. The family arrived in Portland, Victoria in Australia on 25th January 1854. Portland, on the south-eastern coast of Australia, was

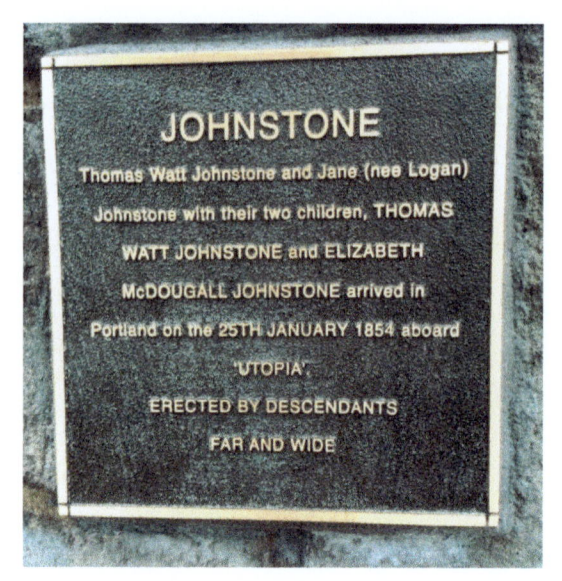

Memorial to Johnstone family landing in Australia.

the first European settlement in Victoria in the early 1800s, set up as a whaling and sealing base.

Thomas Watt Johnstone snr. worked hard, setting up his own business as a plumber, painter and paper hanger, and then zinc worker before becoming the first headmaster at the 32 Common School at Bridgewater, Portland, in 1865. He went on to be Head Teacher at Hawkesdale before retiring in 1892. Thomas and Jane would have eight more children, all born in Portland: John (b. 1855); William (b.1855); Jane (b.1857); Mary (b.1859); George (b.1862); Alice (b.1864); Edward (b.1867); and Francis Archibald (b.1872).

I feel an immense pride for my great, great grandfather, who left his old life behind and helped to educate a new generation of immigrants and created a new life for himself and his family.

A former pupil of Thomas' remembered him in a letter she sent to *The Portland Guardian*,

> *"To the Editor, 'Portland Guardian.' Sir – Your interesting and well-written description of the Bridgewater Back-to-School celebration revived many of my school day experiences, although now 'exiled.' I still happily remember the old school days. Many of the names and doings of the old scholars of school 32 are fresh in my memory. But has not a serious omission been made in referring to the teachers of those days? Surely some of the old timers remember Mr. Thomas Watt Johnstone, the first Bridgewater school master. It is hard to understand a lapse in the memory of the old boys and girls who were taught by the kind-hearted, thoughtful, and indulgent gentleman and scholar. Bridgewater residents who fore-gathered at the re-union, were, I think, sadly lacking in that apparently no reference was made to him, his wife and family. – Yours, etc. R.C. DEAL (nee Aitchison). Koroit, May 14th, 1928."*

Thomas died on the 21st November, 1902 (aged 73) and Jane died in 1916. In 1914, Jane was living with her daughter, Elizabeth, in Hawkesdale. There is a family burial plot in Tower Hill Cemetery, Hawkesdale, in which Thomas and Jane are buried with five of their children, William (1855-1884); George (1862-1889); Alice (1865-1891); Edward (1867-1892); and Francis Archibald (1872-1881).

Finding my Australian Grandfather

There is now a memorial plaque to commemorate Thomas and Jane at Portland on the coast where they may have landed after their long voyage from England.

Their eldest child, Thomas Watt Johnstone, moved away from Portland and headed for the booming town of Melbourne, 200 kilometres to the east. He worked as a Shipping Agent and married Blanche Wallace (born 5th September, 1868 in Belfast, Victoria) on 16th August 1886 in South Melbourne, Victoria. Their four children were Thomas (my grandfather), Alice (Anne's grandmother), Donald and Archibald.

Thanks to the internet and the sharing of information, their lives can now be remembered and celebrated. From my point of view, I feel enriched from discovering their achievements and sacrifices. But, most of all, I feel pride.

The Trail Leads to Scotland

Thomas and May with Archie.